God is Calling You!

Mary B. Williamson

If you wish to contact the Author or Publisher, please Email: storiesforpublication@yahoo.com. After many bleary-eyed edits, if you happen to find a typo, please Email the Publisher who will gratefully fix the typo. Thank you.

Whether you read Christian books, love to color in adult coloring books, or other books on amazon.com or Kindle, please check out the Publisher's website at: www.storiesforpublication.com.

If you like Mary's book, please go to amazon.com and rate her book so others may be blessed by it.

Printed in the United States of America.

Table of Contents

Preface

This book is a refreshing look at the lives of ordinary people whose meetings with Jesus of Nazareth are recorded and their place in history has been forever fixed in the pages of the New Testament. It is believed they were all real people, though not all are named. They share a common experience--a brief but life-changing encounter with the One who knew them intimately--God's own Son. Jesus reached out to each individual on the most personal level imaginable and caused a change so dramatic that their lives were never the same. Today we still hunger for that personal experience. This book is an attempt to show that He is still anxious to meet us today, and not only meet us, but call us His friends.

Forward

"Henceforth I call you friends..." John 15:23

This book is an introduction to a person who is called, "Jesus of Nazareth", "the Promised One", and "the Messiah". We will examine illustrations of how Jesus related to specific individuals in the New Testament Gospels (Matthew, Mark, Luke, and John) so that we may better understand how God is reaching out to us on a personal and individual level today. Romans 1:17 says: "The Gospel reveals how God puts people right with Himself." Jesus' ministry on Earth can be described in just those words--"To put mankind right with God". We are living in a time unlike any other since the beginning of history. The events of September 11, 2001 threatened our Western values and way of life. We now fear horrific attacks of violence and impending war. People need to know that God is there for them, not in the abstract but in reality. His desire is to have a personal relationship with everyone.

As we look at the accounts of various ordinary people recorded in the New Testament, and how their encounters with the Son of God had a life-changing effects, we can hopefully recognize elements of our own nature and identify with some or many of these examples. We will see how God works with our unique humanness to touch us in a personal way. Some poetic license has been taken with some of the gospel characters, but only as a means to relate how similar they were to us modern twenty-first century beings.

Introduction

Most professing Christians have within their spiritual understanding the basic tenets that God allowed His Son to take on human form, be born in poverty, suffer persecution even though innocent of any crime, be sentenced to an excruciating death, and then rise from that experience to a new life and ascension into Heaven. But most of us cannot reiterate what events fill in the gap between the birth and resurrection stories. The four Gospels and the Book of Acts relate many personal encounters between everyday people like you and me with Jesus.

Obviously, Jesus witnessed to large groups. The Gospel of Matthew records instances where thousands of people gathered to hear Jesus teach and who were ministered to not only spiritually but physically as His teaching went long and they grew hungry. But the majority of the accounts are one-on-one encounters where the circumstances of the encounter appear to be almost accidental. But on closer examination, the reasons for the meetings and their inclusion in the Gospel accounts become clear. In every incidence Jesus had foreknowledge of each person and his or her circumstances before the encounter and knew each person with such familiarity that the knowledge had to have come from a Divine source. In John 2:25 we read that there was no reason for anyone to tell Jesus about themselves or their circumstances, because Jesus already knew what was in their hearts. Most of the time there were witnesses to these encounters but they were nonetheless extremely personal, individual, and intimate.

The purpose of this book is to examine these encounters and present the premise that just such a Divine encounter can be had with the Messiah Jesus today.

Jesus desired then and now to call us His friends (John 15:23). The concept of friendship with the Son of God, in effect friendship with God Himself, is mind boggling. It stirs within us a hope that such a thing might be possible. But the natural mind doubts that this could be. So instead of considering the rational possibility of such a concept, let's look at it through the term "grace." It is only through God's grace, an unwarranted gift, that we can establish a relationship of friendship with Almighty God. There is something within the human soul which cries out to be known and understood. It is manifest in our most private thoughts, feelings, and remembrances. We long for something beyond the self; for the Creator who knows us perfectly. We long for unquestionable and complete love. It is that need that draws us toward "strange gods", towards crystals or fortune tellers, towards alcohol or drugs, even towards unhealthy relationships with other people. This longing is a basic part of our humanity and only God can fulfill that need.

The Meeting at the Well
(John Chapter 4:1-54)

The sun was approaching the noon highpoint signaling the time was fast approaching to go to the well before the heat of the day set it. It was another laborious day filled with menial tasks repeated day in and day out. Go get water. Carry the heavy jar to the well. Wait on the man who shared her house and bed while he took her for granted. Never in her wildest dreams would she have thought that a man could be her liberation. For her whole life men had kept her in servitude and submission. She had managed to survive based on this. But it had also marked her as a shamed woman. This is how the world perceived her, but she had not given up on herself. So when she met the stranger that day who knew all about her and still accepted her as she was, she was overwhelmed with joy. Out of the entire population, He had chosen to reveal Himself to her. He did not judge her; He ministered to her.

The woman seemed well aware of her religious and ethnic heritage and the social differences between Samaritans and Jews and men and women. The Old Testament teaches that after the Children of Israel were taken captive by the Assyrians around 722 B.C., the emperor of Assyria repopulated the land of the Israelites with the inhabitants of surrounding Babylonian and Assyrian countries. These people practiced idol worship but also were taught to follow the law of the God of Israel (2 Kings 17). Intermarriage took place between the remnant of Hebrews and the non-Israelites. When the Israelites were allowed to return to the Land, approximately two hundred years later, the Jews of

Jerusalem refused to allow the people now known as Samaritans to have any input in the rebuilding of the Temple. Of course this caused even more division (Ezra 4) which resulted in the Samaritans building another temple of worship on Mt. Gerizim; the very mountain from which the Israelites were to proclaim the blessing of the Lord when they entered the Promised Land (Deuteronomy 11:29). Jesus met the woman at a village known as Sychar, in the vicinity of Shechem. Archeologists have evidence which shows that people were living in this area a thousand years before Abram built his alter to Yaweh there (Genesis 12:6).[1] Today Shechem is most closely identified with the Palestinian town of Nablus and is still the setting for the turmoil of territorial and racial strife.

Geographically Shechem is centered between the two mountains Ebal and Gerizim. Strong[2] defines the word Shechem as meaning "the neck area between the shoulders where a burden is placed or to shoulder such a burden." In other words, it is the place between the two mountains (shoulders) where a yoke would rest. In Deuteronomy 27, we read about Moses' instructions for the various Tribes of Israel to occupy each mountain and pronounce both the blessings (from Mt. Gerizim) and curses (from Mt. Ebal) that God had in store for His people. So here arrived the One who would remove the curse and deliver the blessing to mankind. Here also a woman came carrying a yoke with the physical burden of well water and the spiritual burden of a sinful

1 Markcus, Amy Docksser, The View from Nebo, Little, Brown & Co., 2000, pg. 89
2 Strong, James, The New Strong's Exhaustive Concordance of the Bible, Thomas Nelson, 1990

life. Here she would meet the One who was to say "My yoke is easy."

Shechem is the land that Jacob purchased from the Canaanites (Genesis 33) and set up an altar to the God of Israel therefore allowing the people of this area to claim ancestry through their patriarch Jacob. It is the place his son, Joseph, longed to return to from his sojourn in Egypt and where the promise to bury him was finally fulfilled by Joshua (Joshua 24:32). At the foot of Mount Gerizim is the well bearing Jacob's name. Just as Jacob had met his beloved Rachael at a well centuries earlier, now another woman was to meet a man under similar circumstances with even greater life-changing consequences.

So this is the setting we had: a mixed-breed tribe of people who, according to the Jews, observed an adulterated form of worship represented by an adulterous woman at the well named for the patriarch of both tribes of people. Jesus purportedly stopped at the well to rest, but He knew the woman would meet Him there. When He saw her approaching, He asked her for a drink of water. This went against every social custom of the day—-a Jew should not speak to a Samaritan, a woman should not speak to a stranger, a Jewish man who upheld the laws of purity could not come in contact with any woman, especially one seen as unclean. The woman reacted to the request for water by offering the conventional wisdom of the day. She wanted to debate rules of social propriety and practical issues, but He wanted her to see His Divinity. He answered her objections to His request by saying, "If only you knew what God gives and who it is that is asking you for a drink..." We're the same today. When God reaches out to us, to make Himself known, we react with rational arguments as to why this can't happen rather than seeing Him as a loving, nurturing God eager to fellowship with us.

The woman again answered Jesus with practicalities and doubt: "You don't have a bucket. The well is deep. Where does this life-giving water come from? This is Jacob's well—you don't claim to be greater than Jacob do you?"

Jesus ignored every question and again testified of Himself. One of His own sheep had come there for water and His purpose was to offer her redemption from the life she had led. He reminded her that the prophet Jeremiah (Jeremiah 17:13) described the Lord as "the Spring of Living Water" and that He could provide her with a spring of water that wells up to eternal life.

This statement finally got her attention. But just as quickly she was drawn back into the realities of life. She asked for physical water thinking He could provide a means by which she would never have to bother with drawing well water again. Her misunderstanding of what Jesus was offering obscured her real need to quench her eternal thirst for God. But her interest was definitely peaked by this Jew who had invaded her territory. She was at the half-way point of accepting the gift God was offering her.

Jesus' offer was spiritual and in order for the woman to qualify for it, she must make a confession. She had to lay down her pride and be completely honest with herself about who she was and what her relationship with God was. To her surprise Jesus did not condemn her for having many husbands and living with a man who was not her husband. He spoke to her of spiritual things. At this point the woman could make an honest statement of belief that Messiah would come and "tell us everything." At this Jesus gave the most definite clue as to whom the woman was in the presence of. With reference to Exodus 3:14, He said, "I am He. I Am is talking with you."

Later on the woman returned to her village to share her experience with those who had always shunned her. She told them the exciting news that she had met the Messiah. Her testimony led the villagers to find out for themselves who this Jewish stranger was. It was at an early point in Jesus' ministry that he met with and ministered to the Samaritans, those who were seen as outcasts by the Jews. He told them the wonderful Truth that God is Spirit and it is only by the power of the Holy Spirit that people can worship Him as He really is. Physical location or social status makes no difference. His message was relayed to them through the loving acceptance of one they considered their inferior, the village harlot. Jesus' meeting with the woman at the well was no accident. He sought her out to offer her His love and a new way of life. If He did this for her, will He do any less for us?

The Doubter
(John 1:19-34 & Luke 7:18-23)

John the Baptist (or more correctly called the Immerser) was a cautious man. He was very careful not to offend God; he cared not what others of him. His clothing and lifestyle proved this because he lived in much the same way as did the prophet Elijah whom he emulated. His clothes were made of rough camel hair and he wore a belt made of animal skin wrapped around his waist just as Elijah had done. He lived a sparse life alone in the wilderness, surviving on the land, preparing himself for service to God. While in the wilderness, the voice of the Lord came to him with a commission: "Go and preach repentance from sin and baptism which will lead to forgiveness by God and salvation." The importance of his ministry is defined in the first chapter of Mark as the <u>beginning of the gospel.</u> This "Good News," that the revelation of the Kingdom of God would soon be revealed to mankind, is played out in the life of Jesus of Nazareth.

John assumed the role of the prophets before him; Isaiah and Elijah. He became the voice crying in the wilderness proclaiming the arrival of the Promised One, the Messiah! (Isaiah 40) His ministry along the Jordan River became well known and people thronged to be baptized by John. This outward sign of remission of sin and cleansing was unknown at the time. The Torah had taught that the priests were to be clean before coming before God. God had commanded Moses, Aaron, and his sons to wash before entering the tabernacle (Exodus 40) and the Levites who served in the Tabernacle were sprinkled with the water of purification (Numbers 8). There was also a historical requirement that one's clothes must be clean before approaching God (Exodus 19) when the people were preparing to unite in a covenantal relationship with God on Mount Sinai. But people in general were not required to cleanse themselves as part of their religious observance and in John's time, such an act was virtually unheard of. Even so, the people saw the power of God at work and thronged to John to be baptized as an outward sign of their desire to turn from their sinful ways and eagerly anticipated the coming of the Kingdom of God.

Much to John's dislike, some of those who came to him were the Jewish authorities. They questioned John about who he was and what he was trying to do and he assured them he, himself, was not the Messiah or even Elijah. His response to their questions was to quote Isaiah 40, "I am the voice of one crying in the wilderness, make straight the path of the Lord." From this the authorities should have known that the Promised One would soon be appearing.

The very next day John and Jesus met at the Jordan River where John was carrying out God's command to baptize those who came to him. Jesus approached John and asked to be baptized. John at first refused saying he was not worthy to baptize Jesus, but Jesus insisted telling John that this was what God required. Jesus, ever obedient to His Father's will, reminded the man of John that he must be obedient as well.

Jesus and John were related through their mothers. John's mother, Elizabeth, was pregnant six months before the angel

Gabriel appeared to Mary announcing that she would give birth to the Savior of the world. Elizabeth's pregnancy was a sign for the young girl that God could accomplish anything: an elderly woman conceiving and even a virgin birth. When Mary, who was pregnant with Jesus, visited Elizabeth baby John lept with gladness in his mother's womb.

As youths, the two boys most likely met many times at family gatherings and observances of feasts and holy days, but John could not recognize the miracle living in his midst. It was not until both became grown men that John recognized Jesus as the Messiah. Only when John witnessed the Holy Spirit descending on Jesus and heard the voice of God proclaiming Jesus to be the Son of God did John see God's promise fulfilled.

Even so, at the end of his life, John allowed doubt to creep in. When John's circumstances became critical, he allowed fear and doubt to chip away at the revelation God had given him. John's open stand against the sin of adultery, committed by Herod and Herodias, resulted in his imprisonment. John most likely knew that he would not get out of prison alive. He had been an outstanding servant of God. He lived his life solely relying on God for his existence and defying all convention. But he was cautious of things eternal. And he was human. He allowed fear to weaken his faith. While he was still able he wanted to be sure that Jesus was the Messiah--the Promised One. At one time John had professed Jesus to be the Lamb of God, the holy sacrifice for the sins of the world. Now John's faith was beginning to fail him under the strain of imprisonment and impending execution. He had to make sure his understanding was correct before it was too late.

John had many followers, some of which still exist in the world today, known as the Sabeans. So he sent some of his disciples to Jesus inquiring if He was the One, the *Echad*, or should he expect someone else to come at another time. John, the pillar of righteousness and example of servanthood, had doubts. If someone like John could have doubts, it's no wonder we have doubts too.

Jesus was tender and merciful in allaying John's doubts. His answer to these questions was the same as He presents to those who want to know who He is today. It can best be accepted by those who, like John, know scripture. Jesus sent the disciples back to John with a message that echoed the words of Isaiah Chapters 35 and 61. "Tell John the eyes of the blind are opened, the lame can walk, the lepers are cleansed, the ears of the deaf are open, the dead are raised to life, and the Good News is preached to the poor." And Jesus added a footnote, perhaps for the benefit of the messengers and certainly for our benefit. He said, "How happy are those who have no doubt about me!" In other words, Jesus was saying, "Don't sweat it. Trust Me completely. Have blind faith in who I am and you won't have a care in the world. But if this is impossible for you, search the scriptures and you'll find out who I am."

Loaves and Fishes
(Matthew 14:13-21)

The disciples had brought Jesus the news of John, the Immerser's, violent death. The gruesome details of John's beheading weighed heavily on everyone who knew this man of God. Jesus grieved over the death of His comrade and sought solitude on the Sea of Galilee. He left in a boat, alone, but the crowd followed Him because of the miracles they had seen Him do. They wanted to see more signs and wonders. When He saw the crowd, He took pity on them. They were like sheep without a shepherd (Mark 6:34). He abandoned His own needs, His grief and His need for solitude, and began to teach the multitude who had gathered there. He taught them about the Kingdom of God and healed the sick. Not long before this He had commissioned the disciples to do exactly this and they had rejoiced with Him at their successes. But soon a more practical application for the power Jesus had instilled in His followers would arise. When the day grew late and the crowd became hungry, He told the disciples to feed the hungry crowd. Even though they had received the power and authority of Jesus, Himself, to declare the Kingdom of God and heal the sick, raise the dead, and cast out demons, they did not have the faith to use this power for common everyday needs.

The Gospels indicate that only one person out of a crowd of thousands was prepared to remain an extended time with the Teacher by bringing food. This was a young boy. But who knows what his plan was when he left home that day. Did he prepare his meal or did his mother? Was it food to be delivered to a neighbor's home or a sick relative, or was it merely a brown bag lunch for an incessantly hungry youth? Did the person who prepared the food have some foresight that the meager lunch would be needed for a divine lesson? What a blessing it must have been to know what God was able to do with it! In any case, what a blessing it must have been for whomever prepared that picnic basket to know what God was able to do. But the youth had to be willing and obedient to give up what he had in order to minister to others. Why two fish? Why five loaves? Obviously it indicates that God can take a small gift and multiply it for enormous good. Not only was the small amount sufficient, there was enough bread left over to fill twelve baskets. Is this an inference that in the Last Days the Twelve Tribes of Israel will recognize their Messiah (Revelation 7:4-8 & Romans 11:25-26) and consume the Bread of Life waiting for them?

How does this story apply today? While God could now grieve over the state of the world and the wickedness herein, He instead chooses to recognize our needs and heal us, to nurture us, to feed us, and to meet all our human needs. Jesus' love for the crowd and His disciples that day ministered to their imminent physical needs. This was provided after He had first filled them with spiritual food. So seek out the Kingdom of God and your needs will be provided for. (Luke 12:31)

A Change of Heart
(John Chapters 3, 7, & 19)

Any reader of the New Testament is familiar with the term "Pharisee." The meaning of the term, according to Strong[3] is "separated." In the New Testament the Pharisees were both a powerful and prolific group. Their apparent intention was to hold themselves in higher regard than the common Israelite or other sects of the time. According to Peloubet,[4] it was the Pharisees who were responsible for establishing the oral traditions of the Law which, over time, gained more influence over the people than the Law of Moses. Because they put their "law" above God's Law, Jesus constantly challenged them; however, Jesus did not challenge their authority as teachers and interpreters of the Law; He only challenged the fact that they put themselves above the Law. (Matthew Chapters 15 & 23) In effect, He told the people to do as the Pharisees say, not as they do. He saw them as they truly were and called them "hypocrites" (literally "actors") as they feigned religiosity while always looking out for their own best interests. To the people's astonishment, Jesus told them that their righteousness must exceed that of the scribes and Pharisees, thus exposing the Pharisee's pretense.

That's why the Pharisees hated Jesus so much; whenever Jesus encountered a person, He saw them as they truly were and exposed their true nature. He was the exact opposite of all they taught; the Love of God and the Law incarnate. He displayed God's

---

[3] Strong, op cit

[4] Peloubet, F.N., <u>Bible Dictionary,</u> Zondervan, 1971, pp. 508 & 509

love for the individual regardless of the person's social status or perceived worth.

But as in every group of people, there are some who don't follow the crowd, some who think independently and search for truth even if it means jeopardizing their position within the group. Nicodemus was such a person. He was a respected Pharisee having studied scripture since childhood with some of the most learned teachers in Jerusalem.   His mind had been trained to analyze every angle of an issue before making a decision. He and his comrades took pride in dissecting every Scriptural concept to the nth degree and seeing how many angles an idea might have, often to the point of being ridiculous. There was no true spiritual discernment involved, only critical analysis and abstract therories.

Nicodemus, however, differed from his religious brothers in that he allowed his heart to lead him in decisions as well as his mind. Although he knew and could expound upon every aspect and interpretation of Talmud and Torah, in his heart of hearts Nicodemus desired to know God on a personal, not legalistic, level. Even his name was unique. Its meaning in Greek is prophetic: "*nikos*"- triumphant; and "*demos*"- the people.   In other words Nicodemus was one who would be victorious from among his peers. He was an overcomer who overcame the tendency to see everything intellectually and allowed his heart to lead him into a deeper understanding of spiritual things.

The memory of the twelve year old boy who read the Torah in the Temple that Passover some twenty years ago was never far from his mind. The sounds of the words as the boy spoke quickened his heart. The boy spoke them with an understanding far beyond His years; even with authority. "It was as if he were an eye witness", he would tell his wife, "not an unlearned child. His voice was strong and clear, but there was something more to it. He read with understanding and His understanding struck a chord with my own. I have never experienced anything like it."

Now some twenty years later that same boy who read in the Temple was the man who challenged the priestly system through which Nicodemus received honor and status. This man, Jesus, was seen by the Priestly authorities as a threat to the status quo. But others saw Him as their Deliverer. For this reason, Nicodemus could not resist the opportunity to seek Him out and question Him. He couldn't risk being seen in the company of this controversial man who was perceived to be a rebellious troublemaker. So he sought Him out at night and greeted him as "rabbi;" a teacher sent by God. This acknowledgement opened the door for Jesus to draw Nicodemus even closer. Although Jesus despised the hypocrisy and showiness of the Pharisee in general, He welcomed Nicodemus and enticed him with a spiritual truth, "You must be born again." Instinctively Nicodemus replied from his intellect, "How can a grown man return to his mother's womb?" Jesus then engaged Nicodemus in a conversation predicated many times with, "I am telling you the truth..." He perceived the inklings of doubt in Nicodemus and countered these with physical and Scriptural truths. It was in response to Nicodemus' approach that Jesus stated the

most quoted passage of Scripture, "For God so love the world ..."
(John 3:16)

There is no record that Nicodemus did, at this time, accept
Jesus as his Messiah. Later in his life Nicodemus was appointed
to membership in the Sanhedrin, the council which had legal
authority over the Jews. This tribunal would eventually try not only
Jesus but Peter, Stephen, and Saul of Tarsus, a fellow Pharisee.
It is ironic that Nicodemus would be present when Jesus' case was
brought before this court. (John 7:50) Nicodemus would present
the legal defense for Jesus that an accused man must have the
opportunity to face his condemners before judgment is passed
according to he laws of justice outlined in Exodus 23. Nicodemus
could not go so far as to answer the inquiry of the authorities, "Did
you ever know 'one of us' to believe in Him?" He could not admit
that he did believe, but he did what he could to see that justice
would be accorded the man that had so touched his heart.

There is one more record of Nicodemus in John Chapter 19.
He and his fellow Pharisee, Joseph of Arimethea, helped prepare
Jesus' body for burial. If he was present at the crucifixion, and it is
very likely that he was, the confirmation of who it was who died on
the cross became crystal clear to him. If Nicodemus had any
doubts, they were vanquished when darkness fell at midday and
the earth shook and gave up the dead. (Matthew 27) Now he
made no attempt to hide his devotion to Jesus. He brought huge
amounts of perfumed spices, over one hundred pounds, to anoint
the dead body. His actions could never have gone undetected by
his fellow Pharisees. What was his motivation? It was as if he

wanted one last opportunity to honor the man his peers had so violently opposed. Or did he feel guilt that he had not done everything humanly possible to prevent the horrible death of One who had enticed him to look beyond rationality for spiritual answers? Indeed it had become clear to him and so many others that, as the Roman soldier said, "Truly this was the Son of God."

What a Friend
(John 2:1-25)

In every Biblically recorded encounter between Almighty God and a mere human being, God approached the individual on their own turf, so to speak, and the encounter is always initiated by God, to the surprise of the individual. The accounts of Noah, Abraham, Jacob, Moses, and others indicate that God always initiated the contact. It was rarely the result of someone in deep meditation or any other act of physical or emotional struggle to obtain an audience with God. The setting was always in the person's familiar surroundings and "out of the blue."

This was also the way Jesus came into people's lives. When Jesus met Nathanael as recorded in the first chapter of the Gospel of John, it is obvious that Jesus was already familiar with the young man. At first sight Jesus praised him as being, "An Israelite in whom there is no deceit." Jesus knew Nathanael's nature without ever coming in contact with him before.

John's Gospel is the only one to record this meeting. The other three Gospels pair Philip with Bartholomew when the disciples are listed. The name "Nathanael" means in Hebrew "given of God" so the implication is that John uses the spiritual name for both Nathanael and earlier for Simon who Jesus renamed Cephas or "rock."

Nathanael asked Jesus the question, "How do you know me?" and was astonished by Jesus' answer: "I saw you under the fig tree." Somehow this had great meaning to Nathanael, so much so that this phrase evoked the realization that Jesus was not just some "nobody from Nazareth" but the true, "Son of God, and King of Israel."

The Old Testament portrays having a vineyard and fig trees as symbols of living in peace and prosperity. The prophet Zechariah records the vision of God's Kingdom to come and this peace and security is represented by neighbors having fellowship surrounded by vineyards and fig trees. The picture of someone "under the fig tree" would be someone in communion with God. My guess is that Nathanael was most likely praying and his prayer had something to do with the revelation of the anticipated Messiah. What a mystery that Jesus had such insight into this young man and his private moments.

Does this type of encounter happen in modern times? Dr. Jeffrey Satinover in his book <u>Cracking the Bible Code</u>[5] relates an experience he had when he was in his early 20's. He was alone in broad daylight, enjoying the beauty and peace of a pastoral scene. Then the mood of the moment seemed to change. He felt the unmistakable presence of God. God seemed to be singling him out saying, "Look at my beautiful creation." He was "under the fig tree," communing with his Creator and strongly felt the presence of God. Dr. Satinover's background is scientific, not theological and his book is intended to be a rational analysis of the theory that the Hebrew scriptures contain hidden encoded messages. But the

---

[5] Satinover, Jeffrey, <u>Cracking the Bible Code,</u> William Morrow & Co. 1997

author felt that his private and spiritual experience was sufficiently important enough to be included in his book. His testimony affirms that such an experience is still available to us today.

What Must I Do
(Mark 10:17)

Often we hear God's call to us, but are uncertain about making the commitment we know a sovereign God would require. Our conscience, that small voice of reason that God placed within us, tells us we need to acknowledge God. But our human nature knows the implications of doing so: If we admit there is a Supreme Being, then we must admit that He has higher standards for living our lives than just existing for our own benefit. In order to live a life pleasing to God, we might have to give up some or all of our personal pleasures. Common sense tells us that the hedonistic life cannot be pleasing to a Holy God. So how do we choose to live our lives in 21st century America where every material thing we could ever image can be had? How do we form a comfort zone we can live in where the physical and the spiritual co-exist without interfering with each other?

This struggle of course is not confined to our contemporary world. It is fairly universal, in any affluent society, whether now or centuries before. And this was what the rich man described in Mark's Gospel was struggling with. His meeting with Jesus is also chronicled Matthew 19:16-22 and Luke 18:18-25 with many similarities except for the description of the man himself. Luke says he had some role of authority or leadership among the Jews. Matthew describes him as a young man. He was most likely younger than Jesus, making him between twenty and thirty years old. So the composite of this individual would be a young man of great wealth and status, possessing every material blessing of his day, but hungry for spiritual fulfillment. In other words, a first century Gen Xer. He had everything this world could give and he wanted assurance that that would be the case for eternity.

In the polite custom of the day he addressed Jesus as "Teacher" or "Rabbi" but he added an adjective that Jesus took issue with, the word "Good." Jesus apparently had anticipated the man's inquiry as to what it takes to be "good." He told him there is "no 'Good' except God in heaven". Again we see evidence that Jesus had foreknowledge of the man he was meeting for the first time that day by His saying, "You know the commandments," then reviewing them for him. Indeed the man did know them as he confessed that he had kept all these since he was a child, and Jesus knew that he was telling the truth. He knew that the young man had tried his best to live a life of obedience and reverence and He looked at him with great love. He saw a young man eagerly seeking Truth but He knew that that Truth would be most difficult for him to receive. So He looked lovingly at him and gave the answer the young man found most difficult to accept, "Sell all you have and give the money to the poor, and you will have riches in heaven; then come and follow Me."

This admonition would be difficult for anyone to receive. Clearly the young man had no family to care for or Jesus would not have suggested that he remove financial support from them. Whatever wealth the young man had was his alone to do with as he chose. Jesus required the young man to give up his whole way of life and become His follower.

Since the young man was saddened by Jesus' answer and left downtrodden, most think he did not act on what Jesus had to say.   But Mark mentions another elusive young man who apparently was a follower of Jesus. There was a strange witness to Jesus' arrest in Gethsemane recorded in Mark 14:51. A certain young man, dressed only in linen cloth (perhaps symbolizing the garment used for burials but definitely not the garments of a rich person) was there when Jesus was arrested. He saw the soldiers take Jesus away. When the soldiers saw him they tried to arrest him also but he ran away. They caught onto him by his coat but he ran off leaving them holding the linen cloth.

Someone recognized him to be the rich young man who previously came to Jesus asking how he might obtain eternal life. He had taken Jesus at His word and obeyed Him to the letter. There he was, following Jesus just as he had been invited to do, lacking anything to wear but the simplest garment, as all his earthly possessions had been given to the poor. Once Jesus touches our heart, our lives are forever changed and new directions become a necessity.

The Blind Beggar
(Mark 10:46-52)

The son of Timai was an embarrassment to his family. Having lost his sight, he chose to sit by one of the busiest thoroughfares in the area, the road to Jericho, and beg, drawing attention to himself by shouting loudly. But what he lacked in physical sight, he more than made up for in "spiritual sight" the day that Jesus passed on His way to Jericho.

Hearing that Jesus was nearby, the beggar shouted over and over proclaiming the messiahship of Jesus and asking for mercy. Those around him tried to quieten him but he was determined to be heard. By loudly proclaiming Jesus to be the Son of David, he declared Him to be the fulfillment of the promise made to David in Psalms 89:3-4. It was a blind man's acclamation of what he knew absolutely, without having to "see to believe." And the Lord acknowledged this recognition when He said, "your faith has made you well." Bar-Temaeus openly professed this faith of who Jesus was when was asked "What do you want me to do for you?" He answered, "Teacher, I want to see again."

To see again. He had been sighted once and knew how great a loss he had suffered. He also knew that his chance for restoration was passing by close at hand and he was not about to keep silent and let the opportunity pass. In faith he made his request known. Jesus had said, "Ask and you shall receive," and "you have not because you ask not." So Bar-Temaeus made his request clear and Jesus granted this request so that the Father would be glorified. The lowly beggar became the archetype for Jesus' ministry. All who witnessed this praised God.

Behold My Servant
Matthew 12:18

It was God's will that His Son would come into the world as the servant of mankind. In Isaiah Chapter 42 we read the responsibilities of this Servant: He is to bring justice to all nations, would open the eyes of the blind, and set the captives free. Although the Son had all the power of the Father, His initial role here on earth was as the Son of Man, the lowly, rejected and suffering sacrificial lamb described in Isaiah Chapter 53.

It is interesting to see the different types of people Jesus ministered to. Many were weak and poor like the deaf mute (Mark 7:31-37) and the paralytic (Mark 2:1-12). There were others who were people of authority.

The Roman Officer (Matthew 8:5-13 & Luke 7:1-10) was a man of authority and social position. He approached Jesus and begged Jesus to help his ailing servant. He was a non-Jew but obviously believed that God was more than a mortal Caesar or a graven image. But most importantly, he had faith that Jesus could make his servant well. Here's an odd mixture of a man: a kindhearted Roman official and a "heathen" by Jewish standards who believed in Divine Healing. Although he was a man of power and prestige, an officer in Caesar's army, he was troubled by the suffering of his servant. Jesus could very well relate to the Roman Officer. He, too, was in service to a Higher Authority, serving in a land foreign from His heavenly home, surrounded by human poverty and sickness. But the most important similarity between the two men was their compassion for their fellow man.

Being a man of authority, the Officer recognized Jesus' authority to the point that even Jesus was surprised at the man's faith. Jesus used this faith to admonish His Jewish followers, "I have never found faith like this, even in Israel."

Moreover, the Officer humbled himself before Jesus. Politically, although he had control over Jesus and all the Jews of Judea, rather than flaunting his authority and commanding Jesus to obey him, he chose to say that he did not even deserve to have Jesus come into his house. He had faith that at Jesus' command, even from afar, his servant would be healed.

Jesus met the man on his own terms. He respected the Officer's wish to not enter his house, but did what the Officer asked of Him by healing his servant. When Jesus heard the man say that his servant was "suffering terribly", He identified with the man's concern and decided to grant the Officer's request. He, Himself, became the servant of the Roman Officer and all who came to Him for healing and restitution.

Jairus, an official of the synagogue, was another man of authority. (Luke 8:40-56) And like the Roman Officer, he also humbled himself before Jesus. He literally threw himself at Jesus' feet and begged for the healing of his sick daughter. Jesus did not hesitate to help the man and left right away for Jairus' house. On the way, the news arrived that the daughter had died. Jarius had come looking for Jesus with faith that Jesus could make his daughter well. Then the world intervened. The situation was beyond hope; his daughter was dead. But Jesus told Jairus not to believe the bad news. He told him not to fear, to have faith and his daughter would live. How difficult this is, to have faith in God's promises when the real world tells us there is no hope.

When the terrible news came, Jairus' friends admonished him not to bother the Teacher any longer. Sometimes we get this same bad advice when we need to pray most earnestly. We are told, "Don't pray any longer; it's not God's will, give up." But God honors faithfulness just as in Jairus' case.

Jesus ignored the report and continued on to Jairus' house taking Peter, James and John along. It is interesting that these particular disciples were chosen to accompany their Lord and be witnesses to an astonishing miracle. Jesus certainly didn't need their help in healing the girl. He separated them from the crowd of unbelievers and chose them for a specific reason, to give them an introduction to the Power which had called them away from their daily lives to follow Him. They were about to witness the dead coming back to life! In a few more days these same three disciples would witness an even more amazing event, Jesus' transfiguration, and become privy to the knowledge of who He really is--God's own Son, and what His purpose on earth was, His impending death and resurrection. It was also these three whom Jesus chose to accompany Him as He prayed in the Garden of Gethsemane before His arrest. (Mark 14:33)

When Jesus arrived at Jairus' house, He told the mourners that the girl was not dead, only sleeping. Of course this was met with great ridicule. Jesus took Jairus, the child's mother, and the three disciples in to the girl's room, took her hand, and told her to get up. To the astonishment of all present, the girl arose immediately and began to walk around. The joyful parents were told to get the child something to eat; proof that she was living flesh, not an animated ghost of the child they loved.

The trip to Jairus' house was briefly interrupted by a woman's touch. (Luke 8:43-48) Being an obedient Jew, Jesus wore the *tsi-tsit* or tassels on the corners of the edge of His outer garment. According to Numbers 15, these were meant to be mnemonic devices to remind the wearer of God's love and jealousy for the wearer and to remind the wearer to keep God's commandments. Torah teaches that a bleeding woman is unclean and a devout male Jew should have no contact with her. The woman surely knew of this rule so chose to only touch the edge of His clothing thinking He would not notice it. In order to touch the fringe she had to be almost prostrate behind Jesus. She had to bow so low that her bodily posture put her in complete submission to and at the mercy of whomever she was near. Her plan was secretive—"I know He has the power to heal. If I stoop low enough and touch the outermost point of His garment, I will benefit but He won't even know." But He was aware of her touch to the point of being disturbed by it; He felt power go out of Him as she was immediately healed and questioned the crowd surrounding Him to find out who had touched Him. When the woman finally confessed His reaction surprised her. He told her, "Your faith has made you well, my daughter. Go in peace." God knows our needs. He feels it when we reach out to Him and He answers in love.

All the healings Jesus did were signs of prophetic fulfillment. In most cases Jesus told the witnesses, to the healings, to keep the events to themselves; to "tell no man." Human nature, of course, prevents such a thing. When Jesus healed the leper recorded in Mark 1:40-45 He said to him: "Tell no man, but to go to the priest and offer the sacrifice that Moses ordered." Jesus was referring to the Torah portion in Leviticus Chapter 14 which prescribes the steps involved in ritual purification. The question is, *"when in history had this ever happened before"*? Leprosy was known as the dreaded skin disease from which there was no cure and usually resulted in the exile of those afflicted. So, when had anyone appeared before a priest for examination of the cleansing and then gone through the ritual of purification set down by Moses? What a witness this would have been to the High Priest. He could interact with the healing circumstances and partake of the miracle along with the healed leper. Instead, the leper disobeyed Jesus' admonition and spread the news far and wide. Every such disobedient act put Jesus more and more in harm's way of the Jewish officials. Each miracle He performed caused more fear to grow in their hearts as they feared loosing their control over the people and thus their political standing. But as God's obedient Servant, Jesus could do no less than live His life in service to others.

Dinner with Zacchaeus
(Luke 19:1-10)

Being a servant of others is not always difficult; it can sometimes bring great joy.

Zacchaeus was a very small man in physical stature but carried a lot of weight in the area where he lived and worked in and around Jericho. As chief tax collector he ranked highly among the Romans for whom he collected the taxes from his fellow Jewish countrymen. His occupation of choice was a burden on others but it had made him a rich man and caused him to be despised by his countrymen.

But his spirit sought to please God and it was Zacchaeus' heart's desire to see Jesus in person. When he heard that Jesus was traveling close by he was so excited and eager to get a glimpse of him, that he ran ahead of the crowd which surrounded Jesus and did something very uncharacteristic of a tax collector; he climbed a tree in order to see the One who promised to be his Redemption. Jesus singled Zacchaeus out of the crowd and called to him, "Hurry to me," because today I am coming to dwell with you." Wow, what a statement!

The crowd was outraged that Jesus would speak to this man they termed "a sinner", let alone be his house guest. But Jesus knew Zacchaeus' heart and saw the joy in his face. At that point, Zacchaeus was brought to repentance or *t'shuva*, "I will give half of my belongings to the poor, and if I have cheated anyone, I will pay him back four times as much. The Torah (Exodus 22) teaches that a double repayment is necessary if one takes another's property unjustly, but Zacchaeus wanted there to be no doubt of the sincerity of his repentance so he offered to double what the Law required of him. It was not a mere verbal gesture to win Jesus' approval, but proof of where his heart was. Jesus stood up to the admonitions of the crowd saying, "Today salvation has come to this house... The Son of Man came to seek and to save the lost." Zacchaeus was overjoyed. The One he had gone to find had just said the He had come seeking him. And it was his great honor to serve as His host for the evening.

The Lame Shall Walk
(John 5:1-47)

Jesus returned to Jerusalem to observe one of the Holy Feasts. We are not sure which one, but it was most likely one of the three where it is stipulated that the faithful gather in Jerusalem. These are Passover, First Fruits and Tabernacles (Deuteronomy 16:16). It was not Passover, as the occurrence of Passover was mentioned in the second chapter of John's Gospel.

Arriving at Jerusalem, Jesus entered through what is known as the Sheep's Gate. This was an unusual way to enter the city. Jesus was not literally a sheep herder so he was not there to sell sheep. It was not Passover so he was not there to buy a sacrificial lamb. He appeared there as a sign to proclaim Himself to be the Lamb of God as John, the Immerser, had labeled him twice before. Then He went much further. To the extreme annoyance of the Jewish priestly leadership, the events about to unfold would result in Jesus' declaration that YAHWEH, the Holy One of Israel, was His Father, thus equating Himself with the Father.

Don't ever let anyone try to convince you that Jesus never claimed divinity. In John 5:17-47, Jesus makes it very clear to those who know the scriptures that He is the promised Messiah. He uses material from the prophets: David, Daniel (Daniel Chapters 7, 9 & 12), Isaiah, and Moses as witnesses to prove His identity. Indeed He uses another witness, John the Immerser, only because some of the leaders respected John. Jesus rightly said He did not need human testimony as the Father had given ample information in the Scriptures in order that those who love God could recognize the Son. This is still the best way to discover His identity today.

There was pool near the Sheep's Gate known as Bethesda or Bethzatha—a term meaning "a bubbling up or stirring of the water"[6]. Here the blind, lame and paralyzed gathered to wait on the stirring of the water in belief that the first person to enter the water, when it began to stir, would be healed. What was about to happen at Bethzatha could be seen as the supernatural interfering or "stirring" with the natural resulting in a miraculous result. But the supernatural came from God, not a superstition.

Jesus knew of a man there who had been sick for over thirty years, longer than Jesus had been on Earth, and singled him out from among the crowd. He looked on him with mercy and asked, "Do you want to get well?" That seems like a question with an obvious answer. Of course he wanted to get well or he wouldn't have been there day after day waiting for a miracle. But Jesus wanted the man to ask Him for help. God wants us to make our requests known to Him. With human frailty, the man explained that the reason he wasn't well was because he had no one to help him get in the water; that others rushed in ahead of him every time the opportunity for healing arose. Perhaps he was looking to Jesus to pick him up and place him in the water. But Jesus totally bypassed the "conventional" way of healing at this place. He demonstrated that He was the Divine Healer, not some superstition concerning a bubbling pool of water. He merely commanded the man to take up

---

[6] Edersheim, Alfred, The Life and Times of Jesus the Messiah, Hendrickson Publishers, 1997 , p.320 & 321

his bed and walk. Amazingly, the man did not question Jesus' authority or doubt that he was healed. He *immediately* got up, picked up the mat he had lain on for years, and walked away from the place and circumstances that had held him prisoner for thirty-eight years.

Now let's examine the cripple at the pool. Indeed, Jesus was loving and merciful to the man as he chose to heal that individual from among the many "blind, lame and paralyzed" waiting there. Jesus' choice was not a random one. Once again, He knew the man's spiritual condition long before they met face to face. Apparently the man's spiritual condition was just as bad off as his physical condition, and true to human nature, the one fed off the other. Jesus knew the man's heart—-that he would end up betraying Him to the Jewish leaders. Nonetheless, He chose free this man from the prison of superstition and illness.

The man made his appeal to Jesus in a very pitiable way: "No one will help me,...people get in my way and interfere with me getting into the water,...poor me, poor me." The man took little or no responsibility for helping himself; a perfect candidate for Jesus to demonstrate how God works.

The "work" that Jesus was accused of doing on a Sabbath (which was here is most likely a Feast Day, not the last day of the week as so often taught) was the command: "Stand up, take your mat, and walk." The priests had taken the legalism of not working on a Sabbath to the extreme that one could not even carry a burden on the Sabbath. They immediately accused the lame man of breaking the Law by carrying his mat away. So in order to get the focus off of himself and his "sin", the man turned against his Healer and told the leaders that he wasn't to be blamed for carrying the mat, that it was Jesus who had told him to take up his mat and walk. The man could have responded to the interrogation by praising God that he could now stand and walk, let alone carry a "burden." Instead, he indicated that he had no idea who Jesus was but he made Him the scapegoat. He put his "sin" on Jesus in prophetic anticipation of what would occur at Calvary in roughly three more years.

The timing of the man's betrayal is significant. It was not until after Jesus had found him in the Temple and reminded him of his healing and admonished him to sin no more that the man turned on Jesus. When questioned earlier the man could honestly have said he did not know who it was who had healed him. But after Jesus touched his heart with the commandment to sin no longer, the man allowed more evil to enter his heart and went to the authorities to point out that it was Jesus who had "sinned" by healing on the Sabbath. Had the leaders known the scripture, "the lame shall walk," they would have recognized their Messiah, but they did not relate this situation to the scriptures or correctly apply them to the situation.

Jesus took this opportunity to let them know with Whom they were dealing and the truth of their own spiritual circumstances. The reader is encouraged to carefully study John 5:19-47 to discover what Jesus said about Himself in relationship the Father. Earlier

His words, "My Father is always working," (even on a Sabbath) and I, too, must work" were enough to provoke murder in the hearts of the Jewish authorities. And, "the Father is still working today,"[7] and He wants us to join Him!

---

[7] Blackaby, Henry T. and King, Claude V. Experiencing God, LifeWay Press, 1990

The Blind Shall See & The Question of Sin
(John 9:1-41)

When the disciples observed a man born blind they asked Jesus, "Who sinned, the man or his parents?" This is a familiar question. We often ask ourselves if this or that happened because of this or that previous action, "Did my Dad die this year because I cheated on my taxes?" "Is my child sick because I've been taking money from my employer? If I put the money back will my child recover?" A more difficult question would be, "If I confess my wrongdoing, will my child recover?"

How is sin defined? Let's adopt the definition that sin is anything that separates us from our loving Father in Heaven. All of us commit sin and the Bible teaches that we are all under the curse of Adam's sin until we accept God's plan of redemption through Jesus Christ. So there had to be an "original sin". What was it that destroyed the beautiful relationship God created and intended for man: the complete and constant companionship between the Creator and his workmanship; the gift of a fullness of life and happiness for man and woman in a perfect world cohabited with a loving Deity? What fractured the relationship and broke the Creator's heart by forcing separation between Him and His Creation?

The answer of course is "sin." Many titles have been given to the first sin: disobedience, self-centeredness, deceit, and many more. I believe these are results of the first sin—not the sin itself. Sin is spiritual blindness. Jesus told the blind man that he had "seen" the Son of Man (meaning Himself). He went on to say that the Pharisees who thought themselves to be so learned were in fact blind.

Sin is also the choice to not hear God speaking to us, or if we do hear, choosing to turn a deaf ear. Rationally we tell ourselves God does not speak to us. We look for our answers anywhere but God's leading. The scribes and Pharisees looked for their answers in the Torah—not a bad place to look, but they could not hear the sound of the living Word—the Incarnate Word of God. Adam heard God say to not eat of the fruit of the tree of knowledge, but he choose to listen instead to Eve. Today in our modern world we have hundreds of sources of answers to all life's questions but most of us refuse to make ourselves available to hear (and see) what God is doing around us.

In the tenth chapter of John's Gospel, Jesus confirms this principal. He portrays Himself as the Good Shepherd who has only the best intentions for His sheep. He knows each one of them by name! He calls them out, then goes ahead of them to safely lead their way. He says, "I know my sheep and they know me. I am willing to die for them. I have come in order that you (sheep) might have life and have it abundantly." Open your heart to Him; He will welcome you with love.

Jesus Wept
(John 10:22 - John 11:44)

Jesus had been bitterly rejected in Jerusalem by both the Jewish leaders and some of the common people. He had gone to Jerusalem for Chanukah, the Festival of Dedication, the Remembrance of the Cleansing and Restoration of the Temple by the Maccabees and the Miracle of Light. Previously, at a Passover celebration, Jesus Himself had cleansed the Temple of dishonest vendors and moneychangers. He spoke of the destruction and restoration of the Temple, meaning His own body, but the Temple authorities had no idea what He was talking about. Now He was confronted by an emotional crowd who pressed Him to admit that He was the Messiah. His answer to their confrontation was that He had shown them by His works who He was. If they had understood the prophesies about Messiah, they would understand who He was. He told them about His relationship with His Father and even used scripture to help them understand. Even so, their intention was to stone Him to death for blasphemy. Earlier it had been the Scribes and Priests who came against Jesus but now even the common people opposed Him. It was the Festival of Light, but the people were blind to the Light of the World in their presence. Their zeal to be "Godly" overcame their ability to see God at work among them.

So Jesus left Judea and went across the Jordan to the small town of Bethabara where John the Baptist had had his ministry.

Here Jesus thought He could find solace. In Jerusalem the people pressed Him for signs, but here Jesus could find sanctuary from the perils He faced in Judea. It was here that John the Baptist had lived and worked and many disciples of John remained here. Because of John's testimony, many of these disciples had come to know Jesus as their Messiah.

Meanwhile, in the small Judean town of Bethany where Jesus' friends Mary, Martha and their brother Lazarus lived, circumstances were developing which would and ultimately result in the Jewish authorities final plot to eliminate Jesus and culminate in the sacrifice of His own life at the upcoming Feast of Passover.

Mary, Martha and Lazarus were like family to Jesus and He loved them dearly. When news came to Jesus that Lazarus had taken ill He prophesied, "This sickness will not result in Lazarus' death. This has happened in order to bring glory to God and it will be the means by which the Son of God will receive glory." There are many lessons for us here. Most importantly perhaps is the lesson that what appears to be a tragic situation to us is many times a vehicle that God uses to reveal Himself. He is in control of the seemingly hopeless situations we face and, as Jacob's son Joseph said, what might be intended for evil, God can use for good. So we need to learn to trust God and not our own understanding, as King Solomon said. (Proverbs 3)

Jesus' prophesy showed that He was so in touch with the Father that He knew what the future held. He knew the final outcome of his friend's illness would not be his death but rather set up a chain of events which would ultimately lead to the sacrifice which Jesus had come into the world to make.

For this reason Jesus showed no outward concern for Lazarus' situation. After getting the news, He waited two days before making the decision to leave the area of safety and return to Judea where His own life had been in jeopardy. His disciples were alarmed by His decision and begged Jesus not to return to Judea and put Himself at risk again. But Jesus used this situation to demonstrate to His disciples, once again, that He was not limited by the laws of nature or rational thought. When He told them that Lazarus had fallen asleep, they were greatly relieved. They did not understand His meaning; Lazarus had already died. They had seen Jesus heal the sick many times before and knew that He could easily raise Lazarus from the sleep brought on by serious illness. So they were heart fallen and confused when He told them that Lazarus was actually dead. What a quandary for them. On hearing of Lazarus sickness Jesus had said he would not die, or at least that's the way the disciples interpreted what Jesus had said. Now He was saying that Lazarus had died and that, for their sake, He was glad He wasn't there with him when he died because that would have caused His followers to doubt His power. The true Son of God could not make mistakes and He would not allow His friend to die if it were in His power to save Him.

The miracle, that was about to take place in Bethany, would surpass every miracle Jesus had performed thus far. By raising Lazarus from the dead Jesus would demonstrate the complete power the Father had entrusted to Him--the power over death itself.

And this demonstration would ultimately lead to Jesus' crucifixion. But before this miracle could take place, those closest to Jesus had to come to recognize Him as their Messiah.

By the time Jesus arrived at His friends home, Lazarus was not only dead but buried. Martha ran to meet Jesus on the way and then confronted Him, "If you had only been here my brother would not have died." In effect she was blaming Jesus for her brother's death. Don't we often blame God when bad things happen? Then with hope she made the statement of faith, "I know even now God will give you whatever you ask for." And He replied, "Your brother will rise to life." Martha answered according to her understanding at the time, "I know that he will rise on the last day." But Jesus went beyond this faith by saying, "I am the resurrection and the life. Whoever believes in Me will live, even though he dies; and whoever lives and believes in Me will never die. Do you believe this?" Martha's answer went against the reality of the day, "Yes, Lord." Her brother was dead and buried, but she now professed her belief that Jesus was not just her longtime friend but the Messiah; the Son of God.

Mary was at home with other mourners from Bethany. When her brother died, she lovingly bathed his body with expensive perfume for burial. Without knowing why, she saved some of the oil which she would later use to anoint Jesus' feet. Martha came to Mary and told her that Jesus was on His way to their home and Mary hurried out to meet Him. Weeping and sorrowful she made the same statement her sister had made earlier, "Lord, if you had been here my brother would not have died." Jesus was moved to tears by the sight of the sorrow of those who mourned Lazarus. But even at His display of love and emotion, the critics still spoke against Him, "He gave sight to the blind man, couldn't He have kept Lazarus from dying?"

Still filled with emotion, Jesus went to Lazarus' tomb and ordered that the stone be taken away. Here, again, doubt and unbelief enters through the door of practicality when Martha protested that Lazarus had been dead for four days and he would stink. Jesus reminded Martha of His promise that those who believe in Him would never die. As a sign to those standing there, He prayed aloud to His Father as He had prophesied earlier, "To bring glory to God and to be a sign by which the Son of God will receive glory."

Then He called Lazarus forth and gave the command, "Untie him and let him go." Let him go from the bonds of death. Unbind him and let him be free to live the life God has for him. We wonder how Lazarus felt returning to the land of the living. Apparently he was none the worse off as six days later he was dining with Jesus. This is when Mary took the opportunity to anoint Jesus with the perfume she had used earlier on her brother's corpse. Unknown to her at the time, she was anointing Him for His own burial which was not too far off.

Most of us have learned that one of the shortest verses in the Bible is John 11:35, "Jesus wept." But why did Jesus weep? Obviously He was moved by the emotions of Martha and Mary but

He knew from the beginning that Lazarus was not sick unto death and would recover fully.

Perhaps Jesus wept because He knew that by raising Lazarus from the dead He was playing into the hands of those who were plotting to kill Him. He knew that the ultimate outcome of His obedience to His Father would result in the surrender of His own life, since such a remarkable event as raising one from the dead would push the Jewish authorities beyond the limit of their tolerance. The crowds around Jerusalem had heard of this miracle and gathered shouting Hosanna when Jesus entered Jerusalem on a donkey. This threw the Pharisees into a state of panic. Raising the dead to life again could only be done by a true man of God. Jesus knew what the outcome of His calling Lazarus back from the grave would be and He was overcome with emotion just as He was in the Garden of Gethsemane as the time of His betrayal approached. His act of compassion and obedience signed His own death warrant. The Jewish authorities could no longer tolerate Jesus' influence and so, "from that day on they made plans to kill Jesus". (John 11:53)

We can draw a parallel between then and now. How like Mary and Martha we are when things go badly for us. Both sisters made same the accusation to Jesus, "If you had only been here, then..." We say the same things now: "God, where were you when I needed you?" "Why did you allow this to happen?" The answer is the same as it was in Lazarus' case: If we confess our faith in Him, as did each sister, the final result will glorify both the Father and the Son. What event do we have in our lives today for which we can say, "This is but for the glory of God, that the son of God might be glorified?"

A Donkey's Tale
(Matthew 21:1-11, Mark 11:1-11,
Luke 19:28-40, & John 12:12-19)

This chapter is an imaginary tale built on the details presented in all four Gospels.

The child tenderly placed the hay in the crib for the donkey and softly stoked the young colt as it ate. He loved the animal above everything on earth except his parents. He had raised it since its birth and knew all of its ways. It was as if boy and beast could read each other's mind. The fact that the family owned the animals was unusual and a source of great argument between the boy's mother and father. The family were not farmers or tradesmen who would have need of beasts of burden. The mother was concerned about the expense extra mouths to feed would bring to her household. And when the parents argued about this, the boy took solace in the love which shone in the young colt's large brown eyes. And this made him love the colt all the more.

The boy knew the circumstances as to how the father came to acquire the donkey. Father was somewhat of a dreamer while Mother was too involved with the day-to-day management of their home to dwell on anything impractical. Nevertheless, Father loved to tell the story of what he had witnessed as a youth in Jerusalem about twenty years ago. The boy had heard the story so many times he knew it by heart, but its full meaning was lost on him. It was just after Passover and most of the pilgrims had left the city and returned home. Father's family was from Jerusalem and it was always an exciting and happy time when the faithful returned to

Jerusalem three times a year for the three appointed Feasts of the Lord. One year Father witnessed a very unusual event. A youth, only slightly younger than himself, stayed behind in the city when his family returned to their home in Nazareth. Father was intrigued by this young fellow. Daily the young boy met in the temple with the wisest priests and scribes. Everyone was astonished by his understanding of the scriptures. And when he talked, it was with authority, as though He had lived the scriptures rather than merely memorizing them. The impression this youngster made on Father never left him.

Every year close to Passover Father retold the story. Then about two years ago Father began hearing rumors of a man from Nazareth who people believed to be the Promised One. In his heart Father knew this was the same young man he had seen at the temple and at the Feasts over the years. Then (two years ago this Passover) Father decided to buy the donkey and bring her home. When Mother demanded an explanation Father merely said, "The Lord has need of it." Both Mother and son thought Father's mind was beginning to weaken. A short time latter the family discovered the donkey was in foal. The boy was delighted but not so his parents. So when the colt was born the boy took full responsibility for his care. The boy was looking forward to the day he could ride the colt. It would soon be old enough for even a grown man to ride so the boy's weight would be of no consequence at all to the young animal. But Father insisted that the colt not be ridden.

After feeding the animals the boy took the donkey and colt outside and tied them to the post in front of the house. Then he went inside to have his own breakfast. When he finished eating, he went back outside only to discover to his horror that the animals had been taken by two strangers. Neighbors said the men had taken the animals with the explanation, "The Lord has need of them." Even though this was the phrase Father had always used to justify having the donkeys to begin with, the boy feared for his beloved pet's safety. He ran in the direction the men had taken the animals. Throngs of people joined him running toward Jerusalem. The crowd seemed joyous and in anticipation of some wonderful event. The boy ran alongside the villagers who began to tear the very cloaks off their backs and lay them in the road. Others were stripping branches of the palms that grew along the road and they spread them on top of the cloaks. Excitement electrified the air but only intensified the boy's fear for his lost pet.

Then the boy caught sight of the donkey and the colt walking alongside. On top of the colt sat a man whose very being exerted humility. He was a stranger to the boy but the crowd seemed to consider Him their King. By all appearances the man was not a King—just an ordinary man with an extraordinarily kind face. The people were praising God and shouting, "Hosanna! Blessed is He who comes in the Name of the Lord." Then the boy saw his father in the crowd and ran to his side. He was just in time to hear his father quote the prophet Zechariah, "Rejoice, rejoice, people of Zion! Shout for joy you people of Jerusalem! Look, your King is coming to you. He comes triumphant and victorious, but humble and riding on a donkey, on a colt, the foal of a donkey."

Later that same day a stranger returned the donkey and colt just as mysteriously as they had been taken.

Within a week the atmosphere in Jerusalem would change dramatically. Jubilation gave way to a feeling of heaviness, of impending calamity. The man whom the crowd had welcomed with adulation would be tried and condemned to a horrific death.

And after the horrible events in Jerusalem, during Passover, the boy noticed a new marking had appeared on the colt's back where its rider had sat. A dark symmetrical crosslike marking had become a permanent part of the animal's coat. And a similar marking is still borne today on a donkey's back. The colt was never ridden again.

Malchus' Ear
(Luke 22:50-51 & John 18:10)

The tranquility of the Garden and Jesus' heartfelt prayer was suddenly broken. The scene became chaotic. The sound of approaching soldiers and guards armed with swords and clubs filled Peter with fear. This had been an exhausting night which had begun pleasantly enough by the sharing of the Passover meal. But the fellowship soon turned very ugly when the disciples began to argue among themselves over petty issues of personal pride. Then Jesus announced that one of them was going to betray Him. He even said that Peter himself would soon betray Him. He talked about His death which was fast approaching. Then came the unsettling act of Jesus washing the disciple's feet. And then Jesus talked on into the night about how prophecy was being fulfilled and other things that boggled Peter's mind until he could stay awake no longer. Jesus then withdrew from the group for private prayer.

This brief moment of peace was suddenly shattered by the sound of approaching soldiers. To recover from the rebuke Jesus gave him when he fell asleep, Peter zealously offered to defend the group with one of the two weapons someone had brought along. Again Jesus rebuked them by saying, "Enough of this!" In other words, "We'll have no talk of violence." Even at this most critical time His followers could only understand circumstances in the terms of the natural world. Peter wanted to literally take things in his own hands rather than rely on God.

The disciples were relieved to see Judas Iscariot at the head of the approaching armed forces. He approached Jesus and greeted him with a kiss. Peter, for one, breathed a sigh of relief. Here was a fellow disciple embracing Jesus in an act of love and fellowship. He could not understand Jesus' rebuff, "Judas, you betray Me with a kiss. Be quick about it, friend."

True to form Peter acted impetuously. Grabbing one of the swords laying nearby he struck the High Priest's servant Malchus, or Melek as he was known in Hebrew.[8] There were armed Roman soldiers and Jewish guards there and it might have served a better purpose to attack the soldiers if armed aggression was needed. But it was far safer to attack the unarmed man sent by his master, Caiaphas, to bring Jesus to trial before the Sanhedrin. Not used to using a weapon, Peter found the sword much heavier than he thought and much harder to control. He aimed for Malchus' neck in a feeble attempt to behead the poor man.   But thanks to providence guiding the blade and the fact that Malchus ducked to avoid the blow, all Peter managed to do was cut the man's ear off.

But the wound had a much more serious effect on Malchus than it would have had on other people. As a servant of the High Priest it was Malcus' job to accompany his master in the Temple services.   He would assist in the ritual preparations for the appointed sacrifices and ceremonies. He knew what the Torah taught in Leviticus 21:16-24: no one with any type of blemish could serve in the Temple. This wound would cause him to be ostracized and banished from Temple service. The pain Peter inflicted on him had many ramifications. He stood to loose his livelihood and his

---

[8] Strong, op cit

social standing. He would also loose the privilege of special service which he revered.

Malchus knew he was bleeding and in pain. What he did not know was that the Savior of Mankind and of his own ear was there in front of him. When Jesus saw the injury, He made the same declaration He had made when the disciples offered to take up arms to defend Jesus, "That is enough!" That statement put an immediate end to any further aggression. Then He touched Malchus' ear and restored it. (Luke 22:51) Even though Jesus was confronted by armed guards and Roman soldiers under a Roman commander, His immediate concern was the lowly Temple attendant Malchus.

The New Testament makes no further mention of Malchus. After being so touched by the Lord, could he have possibly continued to be a party to the arrest and trial of Jesus, let alone His ensuing torture and crucifixion? He, like the forgiven thief on the cross next to Jesus, are the final examples of the extraordinary love manifest in the Person of Jesus of Nazareth. Even when He was at the most perilous point in His own life, a point of suffering and fear and impending death, the Son of God put others' needs ahead of His own. What a Friend!

Who Am I?
Matthew 16:13-17

"Who do they say I am?" Jesus asked His disciples. And just as in that day, we, today, are still making erroneous statements about who He is. "He is an historical figure." "He's like Mohammed and Buddha; a great teacher, an ascended master, a good person." But when Jesus asked Peter that question directly, Peter was unflinching in his declaration that, "You are the Christ, the Son of the Living God." The Lord immediately affirmed this to Peter by saying, "Flesh and blood has not revealed this to you." He didn't say, "Yes, you're right," or "No way man, you're way off track." He saw where Peter was spiritually and met him there. Nothing in the physical world revealed the answer to Peter. It came from his spiritual understanding and his faith. Are you able right now to confess whom you might hope Him to be?

Where are you today? Are you "sitting under a fig tree" or "has someone taken a jab at your right ear"? Have you heard rumors that there is One who loved you so much He suffered as no human has ever suffered. Could it be possible that this One knows you to the depths of your being, your innermost thoughts, fears, hopes? He pricks at your heart gently nudging you to acknowledge Him. But we may "kick against the pricks" as Saul did before he was completely overwhelmed by his encounter with his Savior. (Acts 26:14) Wherever you are, He is close by. He knows your most fundamental needs, the things which wrench your heart, your innermost cry. And being so close, it only takes a small step to reach Him. What are you waiting for?

Conclusion: The Act of Believing
Psalm 139:1-16

We are not born "Believers." The experiences in our lives which bring us face-to-face with the Living God are initiated by Him alone. He speaks to us. Our hearts hear something so familiar that we can't help ourselves from crying out in response to that recognition. It is this experience—this call to our most inward being, knowing us as only we know ourselves, even beyond what will sometimes admit—that instills our belief in Him. It is this knowledge, not we of Him but Him of us, that makes us "Believers."

An acquaintance of mine ran a small business and managed hundreds of people. He had the power to hire, promote and even terminate individuals. For the most part he controlled a very important facet of these people's lives—how they earned a living. He told me he was often amazed at how little these individuals regarded the power they had over their own circumstances. Generally they did not ask for pay raises or specific job assignments. He would have loved to have rewarded good workers with more frequent pay raises or a promotion or a more responsible job but he assumed they were happy with the status quo. The rewards were there for them but they didn't ask.

Are we not the same way when it comes to our loving Father in Heaven? He is there for us and is waiting to give us abundant life but we choose to go along from day-to-day as if He weren't in the picture at all. Jesus said, "Ask and it will be given to you..." (Luke 11:9) "....good measure, pressed down, shaken together and running over". (Luke 6:38) How foolish we are to live our lives without taking advantage of this wonderful promise. Both Moses and Peter are examples of men who thought God was mistaken when He called them. They were convinced when they came to understand that the One pursuing them (God) knew them on the most intimate and personal level. This call is what our soul desires but only our heart can receive. God initiates the encounter and it is up to us to heed His call. Take the risk. Ask Him if He's real. Test Him to see if He knows you personally. (Psalms 139) Give up "kicking against the pricks." What are you waiting for? You won't be disappointed!

Mary Williamson

Bibliography

Blackaby, Henry T. and King, Claude V. <u>Experiencing God,</u> LifeWay Press, 1990

Edersheim, Alfred, <u>The Life and Times of Jesus the Messiah,</u> Hendrickson Publishers, 1997

Markcus, Amy Docksser, <u>The View from Nebo</u>, Little, Brown & Co., 2000

Peloubet, F.N., <u>Bible Dictionary,</u> Zondervan, 1971

Satinover, Jeffrey, <u>Cracking the Bible Code,</u> William Morrow & Co. 1997

Sekhar, Chavvakula Chandra; Malikipuram 533 253, E.G.Dt., AP, India, 2002

Strong, James, <u>The New Strong's Exhaustive Concordance of the Bible,</u> Thomas Nelson, 1990

About the Author

Being a Bible student from an early age, Mary had her own personal encounter with the living Christ at age 13. As an adult, Jesus' declaration of love for His disciples in Chapter 15 of John's Gospel and especially His statement, "I call you friends," (John15:15) has had a profound spiritual impact on her. It is her desire, with this book, to let it be known that this love and friendship is available to everyone today.

94107095R00037

Made in the USA
Columbia, SC
19 April 2018